CRYSTAL

Ellen Cranitch is a poet, lecturer and journalist. Her debut collection, *The Immortalist* (Templar Press), was shortlisted for the Seamus Heaney Award for Best First Collection 2018. Her second collection, *Crystal*, was published by Bloodaxe Books in 2024. Born in London of Irish parents, Ellen holds an MA in English Literature from Cambridge University and a PhD in Creative Writing (Poetry and Poetics) from the University of St Andrews. She has taught Creative Writing and literature at a number of universities including University College London and Bath Spa. Recent posts include Lecturer in Creative Writing at the University of Hull where she ran the poetry modules. Her arts journalism has appeared in *The Times*, *The New Statesman* and *The Irish Times* and she contributes poetry reviews and interviews to *Poetry London* and *The Poetry Review*. She currently works at the City Lit Institute, London, teaching the Masterclass and Advanced Poetry Workshop.

ELLEN CRANITCH

CRYSTAL

BLOODAXE BOOKS

ISBN: 978 1 78037 697 4

First published 2024 by
Bloodaxe Books Ltd,
Eastburn,
South Park,
Hexham,
Northumberland NE46 1BS

www.bloodaxebooks.com
For further information about Bloodaxe titles
please visit our website and join our mailing list
or write to the above address for a catalogue.

Supported using public funding by
**ARTS COUNCIL
ENGLAND**

Cover design: Neil Astley & Pamela Robertson-Pearce.

Printed in Great Britain by Bell & Bain Limited, Glasgow, Scotland, on
acid-free paper sourced from mills with FSC chain of custody certification.

CONTENTS

Bonnard I

Four canvases of drowning green, grass so deep,
so apple-filled, it overwhelms,
lead me to that strange image I must own:
the limpid figure in the oval water,
her blurred, elusive features and those planes of light.
She slips between the histories, intangible.
Her names as fitful as a flare-lit river,
her life, the transience, distilled, he sought.

He has trapped her in amber; he has forever
fixed her flux. She is all iridescence.
Her body, weightless, passive, floats in time.
The slim hands drift: but, still, her grip is strong.
She is the blue of evening and the lemon of mimosa.
She is the lilac echo of a yellow song.

Bonnard II

What is that face that plays upon the water?
Whose lambent body swam before his sight?
Is she unchanged now that his art distorts her,
the sapphire figure etched in lines of light?
Ever unstill, she challenges the frame.
Voiceless; she has no mouth to speak her name.

Bonnard III

I pull in at the Musée d'Orsay on a vélib ten minutes before closing, my future and my past unspooling around me, blown through by every breeze that crosses Paris.

Suddenly the note about Bonnard's lover, Renée; she committed suicide weeks after he married Marthe. Now, I cannot choose but see her in every liquid picture, so much dissolution. Her life in every exhibition text; there is *a trajectory of increasing abstraction in his paintings*. It is a terrible feeling, to be becoming less distinct.

There used to be a boundary between myself and the world. Now, the leaf-shape is a blizzard. Now, when I seek out the horizon, it's no longer there. Has it moved to the inside of my mind?

$C_{10}H_{15}N$

Name: Crystal methamphetamine.

Appearance: clear crystal chunks, shiny blue-white rocks, slightly transparent crystals.

Some slang names: ice, crank, meth, Tina, T, jib, shards, gak, speed, crystal.

Routes of administration: oral, intravenous, intramuscular, subcutaneous, vapour inhalation, rectal, insufflation.

Symptoms of addiction:

loss of appetite, weight loss, dilated pupils,
staying up for days even weeks at a time,
borrowing money often, selling possessions,
stealing, sweating, not caring about personal appearance,
elevated body temperature, increased heart rate,
increased blood pressure, insomnia, hypersomnia.

angry outbursts, hostility, aggression,
controlling others,
belittling and criticising others,
intense paranoia, psychotic behavior, intense irritability,
mood swings, hallucinations, homicidal thoughts,
may think about hurting others,
violent behaviour,
secretive behaviour, lying.

*

Addicts...lie to their loved ones to keep them around, to the world to avoid stigmatisation, and to themselves to preserve their drug habit.

– Dr David Sack, BA, Psychiatrist, Addiction Specialist

Words

From the throat of the sky
quick, look,
briefly, it's manifest –
the tumbling snowflake,

its dendrites of ice,
its flawless symmetry.
Words can proliferate
just as suddenly.

Think of how that verbal crystal,
'ice', can multiply;
how it packs into 'malice'
its cold, vengeful heart.

It brings the word closer
to the reality.
There is an intensity
in a word's desire

to become experience.
Concentrate hard,
you might just be able
to feel it –

the elastic reach of language
as it strives for exactitude;
as it attempts to become
not merely to represent.

Strickeen

Where does it come from, the strung-out cry of the mountain's name?

The car has come past, it is holding its course, probing its way through the light-starved interior. Loops of mist puzzle the headlamps, wrestle the beam, as the car pushes through on the single road through the dark valley. Is it her imagination or as the car picks up speed, do the flanks of the mountains edge closer, do they crowd its grey exterior?

Flashes of black, wet-black, the Black Valley's black water. Ropes of anguish. Headstrong the river. Bridles, fretful, thrashes its mane, rises up, channels a voice, a voice to protest, only to crash, fall, break, on unforgiving rock.

The passenger/She, is strapped in. Something had caused her to hesitate before placing the metal plate in the red buckle. He had started to drive faster, faster. He had started to speak slower, slower. His tone, level, like the road. Immaculate, his honed aggression. With the speed, the verbal assaults intensify. Terror takes hold of her. She digs her fingers into the seat. There is nowhere to go. A mind can be placed in the vice of another mind and the screw tightened at the same time as a personality is prised apart.

The road's wetter, closer to the water. As he hits the brake, the car comes to a halt. She feels a jarring pressure – the strap against her chest. Her spirit breaks like surf against the belt.

Actaeon

All that he knows he is, his sense of self, knelt.
He lowers his life, his long-stemmed stag's limbs.
Around him, the forest floor, above, a mauve scent –
chalk-blue elderberries, he tries to reach but can't,
the dogs' bloody teeth in his hide, on his neck,
dragging it down. His tongue, useless, a root;
the light in his eyes, fading now, a dumb plea.
A last time he tries to lift up his head; and feels

the airy scaffold, the pure braced weight of bone;
the wonder of the branching concave crown,
the entire antler edifice move as one
and like an open hand, a hunter's glove,
flare out, to catch and hold an instant
the human voice that she had taken from him.

Metamorphoses

The body is altered but the mind remains the same. Language can't remain neutral. It sculpts itself into conditionals, allows itself to feel, alongside the protagonist, the intensity of their grief.

If words would just have come she would have spoken.

To know you have a voice then know it has been taken away from you.

Io

flat cow skull-bone trying to feel through coarse fur
his knuckles against her brow, the stroke-soft soothe-speak;

flat cow skull-bone gathering all thought, all nerve to accurately feel,
re-feel, focus, the small girl memory of his musk man-smell

when brush of his fingers on her hot forehead would soothe her;
flat cow skull-bone housing gold eyes, gold brimming wet,

black-lashed water, dripping gift-tears onto his hands: *this one is sad*,
says the father. Dull curved cow horns glance at air, turn wide

empty circles, want to link the once-known of arms with his
which reach up to soothe her; stout cow neck's throat-choke

when he offers her the sweetest blades of bitter grass knowing
cow tongue's stoat body squats inside her, cannot be lashed

into supple word-sound. Small word, smallest in the long poem,
carrying on its slight frame the whole yoke of utterance and desire

gifting the soon-to-be exiled poet a longing to shape into words,
into a dazzling white meadow of words to sing of words' torpor.

Uplift

You can be ambushed by happiness at the same time as by hurt.

My elder son Tom calls me from Isfahan. His words trip over themselves in a rush to embrace. During this period of terrorised confusion and dread his calls are comets whose fiery trails I cling to. They deliver me to a rarer air.

Tom

You are the blue that pools, bright as wet pebbles,
in the inked letters on your bedroom wall.
It does not fade, the blue felt-tip on white wallpaper.

You are a white falcon in blue air,
the grace of its moves and its warm, feathered heart.
Its curving wingtips are the contours of your voice

that loved voice which comes to me
from Tehran, from Tashkent
on the breath of the winds that divide us

the dry Sirocco, the dusty Shamal,
which brings whispered hosannas of cypress and pine
and the songs of the great sand-seas.

You are the depthless blue when light leaves the dunes
and I can hear the smallest starts
and shivers of shifting sand

as the mounds of glittering grains lift up
their hems, studded with quartz-dust and light,
shake them out and resettle.

You are ultramarine, the blue of ultimate things,
of fierce risk, of a love that holds nothing back,
that brings all of its faith to remote lands and strangers

and when you call me from Cairo
en route to Khartoum
you are the White Nile and you are the Blue.

Though I can't take your hand, I can still trace its movements
in the words of Raymond Carver on your wall:
I follow your touch in the curve of the 'B',

in the light downstroke pressure of the 'L';
I follow your truth in the word you chose always
to have with you, which you give to me now: *Beloved.*

Athens I

Sometime before the revelations: travelling into the city by night, lights high to the left mark the hill of the Acropolis. I'm thumbing through my old copy of Cavafy and now I understand his poetry: how, like a crystal, where the smallest individual unit has an identical structure to the greater whole, the poems are microcosms that evoke a larger, parallel subject; his own sense of decline, and longing as he aged to regain a vibrant, passionate past, a symbol of Alexandria, now in decay but once fabulous, tumultuous, extravagant. Interiors, walls and shadows frame the verse but it's shot through with lines of transcendent beauty; rhapsodies of tenderness for the bodies of the young killed in war, promises that all the blood and the dust will be washed away, the wounds of battle closed.

Athens II

We're in a hotel room off the city centre. Outside, homeless dogs roam the forecourt of an unopened Costa. Tinsel swings, catching splinters of thin, winter light. In the distance, raucous voices of dockworkers celebrate loudly following a victory for Olympiakos. Suddenly he is a different person. He tries to prevent me calling my children, my brother. He says I am playing 'our sons' off between us; he accuses me of being devious and says I am forcing him to have to control me.

Where are they now, the words to hold me, to assuage?

To Cavafy

Dusk falls in a room off Syntagma Square.
The shadows converge in the low winter light.
Your words are her balm; may they come to her there.

The lines from Cavafy recur like a prayer
pervading her mind when his anger ignites.
Dusk falls in a room off Syntagma Square.

A comb of pearl straightens the raven-black hair
of Sarpedon, dead; dark, those eyes of jadeite.
Your words are her balm; may they come to her there.

Let tears of ambrosia temper the air,
sunbursts of tourmaline hold off the night.
Dusk falls in a room off Syntagma Square.

The rooms where you found love were shadow-filled, bare.
Revived in your lines, they are legendary, bright.
Your words are her balm; may they come to her there.

The terror and hurt, the loss and despair
can be wholly transformed. Words have that might.
Dusk falls in a room off Syntagma Square.
Your words are her balm; may they come to her there.

Revelations

When the revelations finally come, Dan is packing for his last year at Bristol and Tom's in Uzbekistan.

There is too much to take in. I've never felt such an absence of a future, so radical a need to re-evaluate what I thought was the past.

Come to Samarkand, says Tom and I consider it.

Secrets

He tells me he is a drug addict, that he's been addicted to cocaine for about ten years. This is true but it is also a lie because it is not the whole truth, which is that he is also addicted to crystal methamphetamine. He tells me that he is bisexual and that he had a relationship with a man before we married. He has not mentioned this through the years of our marriage. His face as I look at it is not the face of the person I know. He is receding, a stranger. At the same time, my sense of who I am is disappearing. He tells me he is seeing men for sex regularly and has been for several years. He does not tell me he is HIV positive. Neither of us yet knows.

As I move towards my bike, he tries to kiss me.

Seared onto my retina are sexually explicit images, the feel and smear of them; secrecy's livid stain, its putrid stench. What has it tasted, the warm inside of his mouth that I have kissed?

I drag my bike upright, steer it away. Metal on metal, the chime of my ring on the frame.

Our rings are the only two of their kind. They are silver, inlaid with thin, diagonal stripes of gold.

Void

How does a word sound
when it lands

                soundlessly

casts no shadow
speaks unheard?

How does the mind know
to let

                the shield
                    slide over

faced with a knowledge
too great
to be absorbed?

Betrayal

The crystal of cyanide found in the heart
after death by cyanide poisoning.

A cold, sharp-edged mineral buried deep
in the warm, blood-washed muscle of the heart.

The Wishing Cup

He knows this land, its neon glare; each day, the rhythmic sift through stiff, compacted clay. This bare escarpment, taut against a sky of hard blank blue, presses against his eyes even in sleep. So many years now he's been searching. Then yesterday, the boy's foot found the step, a stumble into dust and hope arising like a debris cloud whips up his faith, a faith so threadbare it could snap. That it might be intact, the tomb.

He descends into the chilly dark, strikes a match to test the air, looks in and sees – the warm glow of gold that flows like the Nile through the chamber; eyes kohled in obsidian, amulets, faience, red jasper; the bronze of the flame on silent, sculpted forms, and in front of them all, commandingly, an alabaster chalice shaped like a lotus blossom. An alabaster chalice carved from a single piece of white calcite crystal.

Did he recognise its act of utterance; its palm-of-the-hand-raised *Go no further?* Did it slow and confuse the intruder and delay the plunder? Did it trouble Howard Carter's vision? Calcite splits the light in two: it gives rise to double images.

Double Exposure

A shutter opens and snaps one reality, simultaneously snaps another. I turn my head one way and see one set of facts then turn the other way and see another. The turning is like a fraying or a wrenching. I cannot trust either perspective.

The first is what I thought my relationship with him was; who I thought he was; what I hoped for; how I look back at our shared experience, as students, in love, travelling, bringing up our children, with his family, my family and our friends.

The second is what my relationship with him possibly is; who he really is; what in fact constitutes our relationship – abuse, aggression, betrayal; his making our children complicit in his secret. Are these caused by his drug addiction or not, or not entirely, or not much?

Somewhere in the gap between the two, I am mourning a future and a past. A real, lost past. An imagined past which never was. A love which sometimes was and sometimes was not. I am seeing the conviction we could mould this life disintegrate. I am grieving for my idealism, seeing my belief in the exceptional quality of our relationship shatter, watching that reach into three dimensions, as it colours the past, redefines and remakes it, as it encompasses the future, as it corrodes my present.

Heston Services

Filling the car with petrol at the start of the drive to Bristol.
My younger son, Dan, in the shop buying water.

Suddenly as I sit back inside, the tears,
the readiness of their release,
grief allowed to come and such a swell, a drenched language.

The Drive West

A volatile sun; the yellow of the earth's rim
turning to deep orange.
I am driving with Dan into the last light,
trying to get to Bristol before dark,
and the red disc begins rapidly
to sink, drawing to a close a late September day
and giving a last illumination to the landscape –
the lush oaks near Marlborough,
the dip I'd normally view in daylight –
now, at dusk, tantalisingly strange
with the cross-hatch of street and house lights.

Last night just to see him after all he had revealed
elicited such intense anger and hurt.
Today, it has taken hours to get out of London.
But the healing of the long drive west –
the drive itself was purpose.
We were primed at the promising horizon, shedding.
The beauty of the dusk accompanying the ending
of a part of life. But the skyline extending,
offering more. Dan silent beside me
looking at the firesky, at the world opening out,
as we drove towards the rite of passage of his final year.

Kingsley Road

When I arrived with Dan into his third-year student house he was moving furniture around, chatting, sorting, hanging his clothes. I was listening but I was absorbed, translated, alive to what was happening around me.

Washed turquoise on the walls, a fresco-softness. Sunlight, pouring from the skylight, through the huge Regency windows. Linen curtains, willow-green, abstract patterns, catching the sun's rays. The rustling light, ever at play with the shadow. Chasing, running, racing across and through. The late summer leaves, the way they can express the self in flux. Somehow they offer the fragmented self a place to be and not hurt.

Words from the Bonnard exhibition return to me: *Colour is an end in itself, a way of experiencing the world*. I didn't know then that these colours would recur for me in my office at the university, in the waterlilies, Les Nymphéas, in the Tuileries, and finally at Giverny, in Monet's immersive house, where he woke steeped in flowers, clear vistas and breaking waves of light.

The Stars

He has come in and crashed out, half dressed, on the living room sofa. It is 48 hours before he wakes. I discover later this is the hypersomnia which follows a binge of sex and drugs.

Since Dan returned to university I've taken to sleeping in his attic bedroom. I go there now, pull the cold duvet around me, turn my face towards the shuttered Velux window.

They shine back at me, the luminous constellations.

When Dan was small, I remember how carefully he'd peel the paper backing from each rigid plastic star and position it on the ceiling creating his own celestial nightscape.

They shine back at me, Dan's stars.

Dan

You are my clear water; through all of it,
you kept me sane. Just to speak with you –
I had not dissolved. Just to speak with you.

When you come in at night, bright-faced,
from a music festival in Victoria Park,
you're wearing a khaki cagoule from River Island.

We talk and our conversation is a voice
of its own, strong, free,
urgent as the pealing of bells.

I see colour in the air. It plays, sings, strums.
I see the olive-green of water, straw-green of rushes,
a luminescence race across you.

You are the green fields of Kerry
and their grey stone walls.
You are Joyce's *air and rain and turf and corduroy*

and in those vowels of grace and light,
of space and light,
there is a place I can dwell, reside, be held.

You offer it to me, connection, like a rope,
like plaited twine. When I test it, it holds together,
it takes my weight, it binds.

You are the strong hands that support me
and through my connection with you
I am anchored to life, edged, whole.

Lift me up, he used to say;
always it has stayed with me –
my father's prayer

when his own faith was fading.
Lift me up strong Son of God
that I might see beyond the horizon.

How They Give Back to Me

The touch of the familiar, when the fingers, eyes, caress, and are comforted, then, the mind rests. These are the things: sinking my fingers into the cat's grey fur; the faded stair carpet; the liquid blues and greens that filter light around the living room; the turning leaves of the peonies, tawny, maroon; the slow, climbing progress of the wisteria, the small holly planted for Christmases to come which stands there solidly at the back of the garden, and beyond, the birches with their peeling silver trunks, the sycamore with its ancient crown, its dark canopy. The things I tend and nurture which I have long tended and nurtured: how they return this to me now.

'en las multitudes'

Long ago.
In the garden of a Cuban café in London,
two pairs of green eyes follow me
as I sing 'Gracias a la Vida' by Violeta Parra.

In the bar where we are sitting,
my children have fallen silent as I sing.
A guitarist has started to accompany me.
I pour my heart into the song
which is about the joy of being able to see
in an immense crowd of people
the face of the person that you love.

He has just been talking quietly to me,
voicing the thought,
what if he were to become a drug addict?
And I say if that ever happened
I would be with you in that battle,
give you strength and support.
We would tackle and surmount it together.

His confidence in me is such proof of our intimacy,
the connection between us is so strong.
My love rushes out towards him.
I see a gleaming river, pools of sunlight on its surface.
How fluently it moves.

Much later he tells me that at this time
he was in fact already taking crystal meth.

The river turns in on itself.
Under its skin, the water's muscle clenches.

The Dream

EXTERIOR: *unspecified*

INTERIOR: *Hall of Mirrors*

She moves slowly past the flawless surfaces, through their long, level, yawning away. She's aware of how each thin coating of silver on glass reflects and refracts, and feels it almost physically, the way they stack up and multiply around her. The mirrors contain images that gesture at the facts. In one, a ruby, pigeon-blood red. In another, the hibiscus, its stamens and carpels. In a third, a camera, filming. In the fourth, The Joker and The Ace of Hearts. In the fifth, a scarlet ribbon looped like cursive. In the sixth, curtains, coming to settle; this motion recurring; everything behind them, hidden. She approaches the penultimate mirror, sees – him – but his features are barely recognisable. She advances towards the last glass – to feel herself amplified, to fill the frame. The mirror is empty.

Riverside

Each time, it steals out of the blue.
Each time it takes me by surprise,
To be or not to be.

I love its unheralded, invisible, arrival.
The scene change so inconsequential before it.
The unassuming stage moment as Hamlet wanders on.

I'd left the house in fury, impotent to deflect
his taunting rage, travelled west towards Hammersmith.
A summer evening, the breeze gentle,

the scent, as I round Regent's Park, lavender after rain.
At the end of the performance, I walk out onto the terrace.
High tide, a lilting light, the new moon at play.

Raw, distraught, deeply uncertain, I am connected to all of it:
to the beauty, to the light; to the beauty and the light
which run like veins of fire through Shakespeare's words.

Fife

Before the crisis hit, there was the sense of it: turgid, un-differentiated, a spreading sensation of drowning, of dread. At one time in that time which seemed timeless, fog levelled the pavement from Market Street to Castle House, the sea was a formless grey. Inside of me, something swollen, un-nameable. At the same time, a quagmire dragging me down. Suffocating is directional. When it's in the weft of your own life, it's as if you're in a spider's web, grasping at a medium that entraps you further.

Before the crisis hit, there was a sign of it: a room of under-graduates, wondering – can they get away with not bothering with the semiotics of theatre – how the character of Hamlet is fully realised psychologically, but the characters of Oscar Wilde operate more as symbols, as signs? It occurs to me I inhabit this spectrum. I feel like running my hands over my body to check if there is less of me.

Before the crisis hit, the scene was set for it: Richard the Second, the character, is dissolving, no more than 'a mockery king of snow'. *Richard the Second*, the play, is unrealised, because the text isn't the play's final iteration, it has yet to be performed by actors, experienced by an audience. I'm teaching what I have recently intimately come to know. There are degrees of existence.

'lente currite'

Yet in the final scene of *Dr Faustus*, Faustus speaks in slow iambic pentameter in an attempt to arrest time so as not to slip into the void all characters slip into at the end of a play.

It's a beautiful conundrum – an impalpable character believing only poetry can perpetuate his non-existent self.

'Relapse'

When the hare appears,
it is its stillness
that strikes you,
this cold heart of January
the grass of the dunes
brittle with snow;
its body fine-tuned
to primed attentiveness
which it wears like an aureole
round its downy head;
its front paw, raised,
but ready to be dropped
down, to forge the contact
to propel it,
as it considers the chasm,
the break in the cliffs,
through which the wind
pours, drawing up
the grey strands of the sea.

When the word appears
it is the image
that strikes me
this raw night in February
the greeting between us
stilted and slow.
He uses it freely.
He uses it easily.
But I can't even approach
the brink of the concept
which conjures not just
a headlong descent
into the drugs again,
but the compulsive sex.
I stare at the chasm,
the word-rift between us,
hear the wind roar
as it drives
the grey hounds of the sea.

Like the hare rising out of its winter landscape,
its crystal fur covered in hoarfrost,
the word must remain in outline only.
It must never come into focus.

Bypass

Driving on the North Circular Road, a cold March morning,
the sky, crash-barrier grey.
Adjacent in the car, there's a good chance
we'll be attuned to the frayed edges of the other.
There's a possibility of connection.

Suddenly his shoulders soften and relax.
He rests his fingers more easily on the steering wheel.
His eyes focus on some invisible horizon.

It is as though he moves sideways out of his body,
slips out of his frame.
It is his out of body experience but I am experiencing it.
I didn't know it at the time but this is the moment,
after he had sworn that he was giving up, that he decides to use again.

How did this moment articulate itself in his mind?
Was it a conscious decision?
Or was it entirely passive, a simple relaxation of tension,
allowing the gates to open, the warmth to flood in?

It wasn't a struggle in any sense that I could discern.
It was the decision having been made;
it was an expanding into a coveted and familiar consequence,
like a deep and deeply satisfying exhalation of breath.

Trust

How many times did I ask him, are you using?
How many times did he deny it when he was?

He looks into my eyes as he lies.
My eyes register the lie.

His eyes register my disbelief.
His eyes communicate his anger.

At the perversity of this,
my eyes express rage.

We are trapped in the labyrinth of the gaze.

SOME STATISTICS ON RELAPSE

61% percent of the sample relapsed to methamphetamine use within 1 year after treatment...

> – Brecht and Herbeck, *Journal of Drug and Alcohol Dependence*

...When all relapse incidents are grouped together, ... it is estimated that 92% of crystal meth users will relapse at least once in their recovery efforts...

> – U.S National Institutes of Health

The Undertow

The reactions of others so often compound my confusion
and mistrust, the gulf in our viewpoints, a physical jolt, like
putting a foot out to descend a staircase only to find yourself
plummeting, too rapidly, into the interior of another mind's
biases and sacrosanct beliefs.

The imperative to challenge others' opinions, to constantly
compare and adjust my own, to find again, know again, what
is particular, is difficult and disorientating. I'm no longer
sure that I am right yet I'm afraid of being wrongly
influenced to share their outlook. In these encounters, I
sense the undertow, the tug of chaos, the slow drag back.

I'm struck by the intensity of peoples' response. How, in
this area of unknowing, where so much is still not
understood, there is such a rush to deliver a verdict; and
how, so often, in the presence of the multifaceted and
uncommon, it is the common tendency that operates,
whereby people are unable to see another's situation except
through the prism of their own.

Reactions

You should fight to save your marriage
TRANSLATION:
A 'failed' marriage is shameful.

Will you take him back?
TRANSLATION:
A relationship is something that can be given and withdrawn.

Surely you knew
TRANSLATION:
I am a liar. I am lying to this friend and to myself.

Don't you think you were naïve?
TRANSLATION:
No man can be trusted. Why couldn't you see that?

You're in denial.
TRANSLATION:
I am refusing to confront what's going on.

You should have an affair
TRANSLATION:
An affair is the appropriate, vengeful act.

Kinship

It's not that I don't tell people what I'm going through, it's that I have learned to be wary. Some people I think of as close express a pity that lacks empathy. Others hover on the threshold of prurient curiosity. And yet, the electrifying spark, like a twist of copper wire gleaming, of a true friend; the vertiginous deepening of our relationship, the immeasurable gratitude I feel to those who meet me with compassion, who attempt understanding. Are friends distinguished by how they react to your suffering?

Praed Street

A low-lit kitchen in Paddington. Braids of rain on the fugged-up first floor window. I'm talking to a friend whose ex-partner is an addict. She says all the experts agree that boundaries are essential in this, there is no way you can have a relationship with an addict.

How is it, then, that sometimes you just don't hear? Even when she speaks with all the urgency she can muster, even when she virtually shouts, *you need to protect yourself – your money, your health – he will take them from you...* How come I ignore it?

I am exploded, broken open, singing a song of a pure un-boundaried self.

Outside, the vivid scarlet of rowan berries.

Prayer

I've left the house after another drug-fuelled argument, another psychic assault. 'TOM MIDDLE EAST' flashes across my phone. I pull my bike off Mackenzie Road. Kids kick a football aimlessly across wet tarmac. Tom is gazing from a rooftop at a desert town and a minaret. Suddenly he cries 'Can you hear the call to prayer?' The sound resonates beneath everything he is saying and, urgently, he wants to be sure I can hear it too. Tom is distilled now into a single concentrated force, the desire to share with me the song of faith willing it over so many miles, pressing the phone to his ear, connecting not just the two of us but the prayer through us.

The Beaked Ships

My anger, no matter how vehement, fails to dent his narcotic armour. I have thrown his voice across the floor but there is no relief. The anger curves back. It's exhausting. To be denied anger's release. To be consumed yourself by your anger against another.

The Iliad knows about anger, how it corrodes; the stifling sand, implacable heat, the water smooth as olive oil. The stationary ships.

The ships' curved prows are carved to look like this – their ends hooked like a fisherman's fly.

To Forget

To forget, not think of him.
For that forgetting to grow.

Like the crystal grows
at the fringes of a salt lake.

Is that what I want?

Kryos

Crystal, from the Greek *kryos – frost*; from the proto-Indo-European root, *kreus – to begin to freeze, form a crust.*

The Empty Space

Brighton, February. Mist from the sea moves
blank, opaque, over the chalk cliffs.

I try to do what people suggest – ask others for the support
and advice I used to rely on from him.

So, I ask a friend if I can rehearse for a gig with her.
She says yes. Gamely we have a go.

But as we sit opposite each other, in her eyes,
the faltering, the lack of certainty

the fear that perhaps this can never work,
she is not him. And in my eyes,

the faltering, the lack of certainty
the fear that perhaps this can never work, she is not him.

Each time you reach out to someone else to help you,
loss is what is placed in your arms.

Church of St Michael and All Angels

Early on a winter's afternoon, the clocks, long since, gone back. Darkness, cold, the stone seat in the church freezing my flesh. I have come here because I can be anywhere, there is nowhere and no one that binds me. I have come to this place where T.S. Eliot's ashes are interred because I know with the deepest and most certain truth I hold that the only way through this is through poetry.

The words from the *Four Quartets* speak to me now, they show me the way. They urge me to wait in stillness, in darkness, to allow myself to feel all that has occurred. I have found I have no option. All of the feelings, all of the worst, must be experienced, they demand that.

The church has such a neglected feel. In it, I can't escape the fact of death. Many of the others who have come are elderly and their comments spin me back down the decades. And yet: the inspirational headmistress I would work for in a heartbeat; the charismatic speaker, his boundless enthusiasm and erudition. The woman who had met Eliot. The man who had met Neruda.

In the lines addressed to the soul in 'East Coker' there is a lyric intimacy in the voice. It reminds me of the Shakespeare sonnet, *Poor soul...*, I want to speak to my soul like this, I want to stop trying for a moment, to acknowledge that there is pain.

Let me take it in the palm of my hand, let me cradle it with infinite care, this frail, bewildered thing. Let me make of the shelter of my hands a place of refuge. Let me keep you safe, my soul, through the onslaught.

The Colour of Blood

His boots are the red-brown of iron oxide. My shoes are ox blood red. My feet in the stiff patent leather ache at the toes. His boots are comfortable and well worn in. I am waiting for Tom at night in a quiet street in Paris. He is walking – along mountain roads, through sheltered forests, across country borders – towards me.

He is coming back from Georgia, after cutting short his time in Uzbekistan. Samarkand was too far for me but we will meet here in Paris, following a phone call, when, in response to his question, how are you, I found I had no reserves, I could not pretend, I did what I swore I would never do to my children, told him I was a mess and tears came into my eyes though no one saw.

He arrives around the corner from the Caucasus. I see hiking boots and a thick woollen fleece. A few days ago he was skirting the snowline, climbing through forests of spruce and pine, dizzyingly high, on the old Silk Road between the Black and the Caspian Seas. He speaks of sunlight on bare plateaus, sinuous rivers buffeted by wind and rain. He describes how the volcanic rock of the mountains weathers in the extreme conditions, staining the earth underfoot a rust-coloured brown.

I hold out my arms and embrace him, hug him to me, feel the warmth of his body wrapped in mine, feel the heat of the colour of our blood.

Chez Camille

A bistro near the Marais. Warm, after the chill outside.
Red leather seats and zinc topped tables.
A family opposite. I can't take my eyes off them.

What comes into play is myself over many years,
as a child, as a teenager with my little sister, as a young adult, as a mother.
At the same time I see, as though writ large and illuminated,

the ease of family bonds, everything about them that is precious
buoyant, free. The father is miming, pretending to be
whatever animal the children come up with.

The two sisters are excited, trying to outdo one another;
the younger girl, besotted with the older one.
I see the contentment on the mother's face.

I remember how a mother feels, how a daughter and a sister feel
when they are at peace within their family. All of my selves are in play
and I am mourning the loss of all of them.

I am grieving too for my family, which is broken, for the ties now gone
that held my children, him, myself; for that extra thing we became
at our best moments together. I think of holidays in Sicily

when Tom and Dan were small, and so tired and tousled,
so warmed from the sun, they fell asleep in their pizzas;
when he was speaking Italian and I was so happy,

so in the moment, so much not wanting anything more.
Summer held us in its arms, we were wrapped in the gentlest of bonds,
the ties you hardly notice until they are gone.

Degrees of Separation

On the slope below me, a child is blowing bubbles. It's cold here in Parc de Belleville and I breathe on my hands, rub them together. And instantly I'm taken back – to the wand between my fingers, its brittle plastic; the wafer of liquid, tight as a drumskin; the mobile, mother-of-pearl worlds that flew across its surface; and to one particular memory.

I was trying to extract a bubble from a large bowl of liquid. I learned that there were three possible outcomes. The bubble could be drawn off, detach, float away. Or it could end up perched on the main liquid mass, remaining intact but having failed to achieve full separation. Or, in trying to become detached, it could pop, become nothingness. Later I read that the violent collapse of a bubble, known as cavitation, generates shock waves. It is used in weapons manufacture.

Panic Attack

Like a child whose heavy head hangs down
as she allows herself to drift into sleep
but then a nightmare wakes her and she starts;
her head jerks upright, neck stiffens,
her eyes stare, open, wide –
so, my mind follows,
drowsily, the cyclamen leaf's circles,
its branching silver veins, down, down,
beyond the rim of the corolla.
I find the inner heart, dark as laurel,
bright as wintergreen,
that place of strength where I might rest.
I long for sleep, am almost there – descended.
But the cyclamen, curt, in her hood of pink,
wishes to speak. Her upswept petals rake the wind.
I wake abruptly at her warning:
'All my petals are toothed and, at each flower's base
I have a dark, purple-stained mouth.'

Antiphon

We decide to leave the city. On the train to Normandy, a tiredness envelops me, all-encompassing, bone-deep. But at night, in the airless B and B, I wake abruptly reliving the shocks. Unable to sleep, I google places we might visit the following day. I come upon the Château de la Madeleine.

Arriving there, I discover that the priory with its castle was built by St Adjuter, the patron saint of the river sailors. It watched over them as they lived and worked on the water.

And is it because I am seeking respite so urgently and the Château de la Madeleine with its worn flagstones, mute history and profusion of wild cyclamen is somehow both an acknowledgement and a response, that I find solace in its embrace and in the green, still waters of the Seine?

Tributary

Stand and hold for a moment, the framed thought
this evening's view proposes: the still feel

of the Eure, of this hour, of not being
at a restless urban heart. It lets me down

gently, to a deep part of myself. Untravelled:
for I seldom feel assured the mind will not

dissolve the mind-created self. Spires of song
from the poplars. The doves settle

and in the shallows, bronze-leafed willows trail.
The river has forgotten itself. It is a green view:

the promise of a place where I might yet
unmoored, be anchored, and, mindful, forget.

The Question of Intention

How to think about it, the intractable ambiguity; to what extent is an addict's behaviour an exercise in free will and to what extent is it due to factors outside their control? Is addiction moral weakness? Is it an illness or genetically determined? Is it the product of childhood trauma?

These questions, ultimately so significant, carried little significance to begin with. It was a long time before they became questions it was necessary to ask. The answers, even if they could have been arrived at in any definitive way, could not alter the intensity of the pain felt as a result of his actions: the fact of the sex, of the secrets; the experience of paranoid aggression, the terror of being controlled.

Later though, as time passed, and as it became possible to separate the person from the behaviours, the question of intention became paramount. Different criteria pertain if addiction is understood, wholly or in part, as an illness, or in some way predetermined, or outside of the addict's control.

The Parable of the Emerald and Dark Water

Deep beneath the Andes' peaks
a sunless river flows
a river with a silent wish
to make an emerald grow.

Dark Water courses through the rock
past limestone stalactites
to find the green translucent planes
the mineral ribbed with light.

Dark Water's beaten-silver folds,
her liquid arms embrace
the emerald as she stoops to wash
the debris from its face.

Dark Water gives the emerald gifts
the iron it can't forgo.
Dark Water bends her iron will
to make the emerald grow.

But miners strike the walls of rock.
They hack the carbon seams.
The Green Wars of Colombia
consume their lives and dreams.

And temperatures within the range
must reach the pre-set norm.
Only an incandescent heat
permits a gem to form.

And pressure must be optimal:
the right tectonic stress.
These factors outside her control
all have to coalesce.

So if it blooms, long years from now,
an emerald display:
Was Dark Water responsible?
Can anybody say?

Over the centuries, various narrow 'definitions' of addiction have not helped save lives or made humanity saner or more resilient... The dependence syndrome combines biological, inter-personal and societal ...and inter-generational dimensions...

– *Journal of the Academy of Social Sciences*

Addiction is a treatable, chronic medical disease involving complex interactions among brain circuits, genetics, the environment, and an individual's life experiences.

– *American Society of Addiction Medicine*

Rather than see addiction as a choice that people make – the 'choice/conscious-decision' model, or as due to inherent brain disease – the dominant medical theory –I see it as a complex response to childhood adverse experiences.

Addiction is a psychophysiological response to childhood trauma and emotional loss.

– Dr Gabor Maté, Addiction Specialist,
author of *In the Realm of Hungry Ghosts*

Crystall

'Crystall is a brighte stone and clere with watery colour.
Men trowe that it is of snowe.'

De proprietatibus rerum, 1240

Judgement

I

Pilate: his head heavy, suddenly,
colossal; his palms, films of sweat,
looks like he might lose
his footing, staggers, sways,
his head heavy, with the weight,
the decision, with trying to navigate
the forked path of the judgement.

Bobbles of wool from his cloak's lining
stick to his palms as he gathers the velvet,
throws it out behind him,
making an effort – though his hands
have almost no purchase –
to stand upright,
trying to look bigger, imperial.

For a moment he tries to imagine
how the cloak's sheer waterfall
must appear to others,
how it is perceived for example
by this man before him,
whom he can barely see,
because of the metallic clench of the migraine.

But it is so hard to keep his mind there,
in the mind of another.
He looks down, distracted.
The ground sways beneath him.
The cloak's gilded edge
trails in the dust
making scalloped, hypnotic patterns.

And what might it cost me
to raise my head and turn –
a lithe, easy movement
that barely disturbs a curl –
to make the imaginative switch
in perspective,
the prelude to compassion?

II

Pilate as imagined by Bulgakov.
The pitiless Jerusalem sun.
A fallible Pilate who flounders –
the Aramaic tongue, the stagnant heat –
who did not choose the unenviable task;
who has to choose between Yeshua and Bar-Abba.

Pilate fails according to the Evangelists:
he condemned an innocent man to death.
If Pilate knew that Yeshua was innocent,
if he simply allowed himself
to be influenced by the crowd,
I wonder if he ever forgave himself.

The question spins and rests with me.
What is it to fail in relation to forgiveness?
I thought I knew; the answer clear-cut
as the vertical pitch of Pilate's robe.
But waves, mauve and shadowed,
were surrounding me, suffocating waves.

There were life-saving rafts of thought,
childhood tenets of unconditional forgiveness;
cherished, embroidered structures:
Forgive them father, they know not what they do.
They had once wrapped me in comfort
But now they lured me towards a suspect shore,

towards the action of 'enabling'.
The questions, new, were newly difficult:
Can you forgive when you should not?
Are you forgiving not from compassion
but because it is the easier choice?
Is it an issue of safety rather than forgiveness?

DEFINITION OF ENABLING

One who enables another to achieve an end; especially one who enables another to persist in self-destructive behaviour (such as substance abuse) by providing excuses or by making it possible to avoid the consequences of such behaviour.

– merriam-webster.com

Enabling prolongs the problem by allowing …{a}…loved one to avoid negative consequences that would motivate change.

– Sharon Martin, Psychotherapist, BA, MSW, LCSW

Living with Uncertainty

I

In the midst of uncertainty, how we crave the distinguishing design.

For some time now, we've been living apart. I'm anxious to give the future a shape, to know how things will unfold. Will we separate permanently or is it conceivable we might reunite? I ask myself how I will ever be able to trust again when trust has been so broken. At the same time I know that the hardest thing about trust is how, like hope, it will not die. But the future is unclear; time itself transformed, a recalcitrant, elusive thing.

II

April in the rain forest of Sinharaja, Sri Lanka.
Monsoon winds batter the canopy
shaking the resin trees and Crook Fruit Palms.
This is a liquid landscape
amplified now by incessant rains.
To the north, Ratnapura, the City of Gems.
Here are the sapphire mines
where powerful trunks of giant bamboo
lashed into the corners as supporting struts
reach upwards, craving air and sky.
But the miners are urged downwards
into dark, damp and heat
so as to find the precious crystal.
Suddenly the exhausted shout:
visible for an instant, in the yellow gravel
a glint of blue.

It takes millions of years for a natural sapphire's crystal lattice to form.

April in Guilin, Guangxi region, China.
The fourth lunar month, the beginning of the plum rain.
The yellow plums have fallen to the south of the Yangtze.
Water buffalo graze along the Li river
Twisted peaks of the karst landscape
rise into skies of mist and pearl.
To the south of Guilin is Wuzhou
also known as Gemstone City,
the site of the Fu Rong synthetic gem factory.
Here, synthetic sapphires of all hues are processed.
Some of the most sought-after:
the intense orange sapphire, the padparadscha;
the star sapphire – gems that exhibit asterism –
a star-shaped concentration of reflected light.
But the most coveted synthetic sapphire of all remains blue:
the brilliant cornflower blue.

It takes a few days for a synthetic sapphire to be created.

ADDICTION INTERACTION DISORDER

Cross addiction, also known as addiction transfer or Addiction Interaction Disorder, is when a person has two or more addictive behaviours. The addictions can include alcohol or other drugs, but also addictions to food, gambling, sex, gaming or other compulsive behaviours... People who have one addiction are more susceptible to cross addiction... because their brains are still looking for that feel-good dopamine rush...

– Hazelden Betty Ford Foundation

The term 'Addiction Interaction Disorder' was introduced by Dr Patrick Carnes in 2011.
...Many of these addictions don't only coexist, but interact, reinforce and fuse together becoming part of a package known as Addiction Interaction.

– scientificamerican.com

Dissonance

Later, I would come to more fully understand the nature of cross addiction. Later, I would be able to view the sexual behaviours not as an overwhelming source of pain, not as a comment on our relationship. I'd be able to see them not as singular but as one of a kind – on the same spectrum as the drug addiction – just another compulsive behavior, chasing the same dopamine high. Later, I would be able to wholly subscribe to the need to talk openly about cross addiction because I would know that if you keep silent about these behaviours you implicitly acknowledge that they are deserving of stigma and shame and endorse the idea that addiction is a conscious and deliberate act of ill-doing.

But at the time, it was too hard, it could not be done. My intellect and my emotions were travelling at a different pace – my emotions lagging behind until all that must be felt, had been felt.

ADDICTION AND PLEASURE

Addicts ...engage in their addictions not to feel good, but to achieve a sensation of disconnection and numbness.

– Psychiatry and Behavioural Health Learning Network

INTERVIEWER: Is the addict's aim to get the most pleasure as possible in as short a time as possible?

DR GABOR MATÉ: Not to get the most pleasure but to get the most relief from pain... Addiction is always an escape from pain... The question isn't why the addiction but why the pain.

'Against Hurt'

J.H. Prynne's poem, a rock throughout this time; talisman, companion, lodestar.

In it, it is the lacunae that speak:

> *Endowed with so much*
> *suffering, they should be / and that*
> *they are so —*

The word 'hurt,' with its sharp cry of pain, is absent from the second line. Why does he omit it? Why does the poem move straight from the potential for hurt to occur simply because we are human, to the fact that it does, and it will? There's an ease to the segue, yet there is at the same time a protest against that, a sense of the terrible cost. The unvoiced / is a cut, a gash. It is a black hole, a silent, open mouth.

This is a poem that thrums with pain yet somehow offers hope. Again and again, the way a thought is framed arrests me. I revolve it in my mind, each new idea which comes into being, the novelty of its syntax, the sunlight of each concept. The lines about pain take it from me.

The Ascent

I had arrived at the Colleen Bawn,
the large limestone rock that stands in Muckross Lake, Killarney.
Specifically, I had arrived under it
to shelter from the autumn rain, this possible
because the rock is balanced on a thin stem of eroded stone
shaped like an apple core, its sides gouged out
as though cuffed by a giant hand.

To reach the Colleen Bawn, you have to pad across
the isthmus of land connecting rock to lakeshore,
the clear lake water squelching beneath you.
Bright gills of weed float green and luminescent.
Dark sand churns, and at each step your foot vanishes,
swallowed by soft turf, the dense, brown-black peat
that lies under so much of this Munster land.

You step into a cavern of shadow and light.
Strange, surreal rock formations above and around you.
Water pools on shelves.
Water's reflection plays, quicksilver,
on the underside of the boulder over your head.
Above you, the weight of an entire rock
with the small family of plants that cling to its summit –
whitebeam, arbutus, a few blades of grass –
stocky, determined shrubs that slant like intention towards the west.

The limestone is pale grey, at times, darker,
the colour of pewter, or rain building in urban cloud.
Honeycombed over many years, it has split into caves,
ravines and underground streams.
Glaciers have cut their way through this landscape.
Sometimes there is a gleam, a coruscation of light.
Quartz. Karst. Crystal.

To reach the rock's summit you have to climb upwards
on the inside through the hollow centre
negotiating handholds and open spaces.
I begin the ascent.
In places the surface is pocked, worn,
and my fingers scoop only shadow.
Other times as I reach out, I flinch,
accidentally gripping a rock edge so sharp
it cuts right through and I bleed.

The last part of the climb, you have to haul yourself up
along a slanted rockface longer than you are tall.
You strain to grasp the upper ridge
all the while catching glimpses below of brittle flint
and feldspar where you cannot afford to fall.

Finally I emerge.
This arrow of limestone is sunlit, windy, washed in October light.
The familiar landscape is rinsed, fresh,
the mountains, diaphanous as the water,
the oak canopy, the gentlest of landings,
the sky, achievable.

Beauty

It is long corridors of rain shaking across columns of sunlight,
daybreak, on the Lower Lake, Killarney.

It is a clear night on that same lake when all the constellations are reflected.
And you can see a second heaven. And you can hear the voices of the stars.

It is the hazel ring in adult eyes, the changing green of children's eyes,
eyes that know love like the lake the night stars.

It is the clarity of ice around the apple blossom, a late frost,
how ice holds the bud perfected, on the brink, like the coining of an idea.

It was once an absolute value, up there with Truth and Justice,
one of Plato's Forms; it was a casualty of the new philosophy.

Like the lower arc of the rainbow, hidden by the horizon,
it disappeared from the pantheon and ceased to be of interest to philosophers.

It is being turned outwards towards, as the flower is turned outwards towards.
It is that parabola of hope, that incline and inclination.

It is vivid wonder; an openness which contains within it a readiness to risk.
It is to feel connected, to life, to others, to feel the force

and release of that connection, how it is both intimate and extroverted.
It is what steps in to offer you connection when you are most alone.

It is ephemeral, no sooner felt than fled, *When the trees were there,*
I cared that they were there, and now they are gone.

I have come to understand the power of beauty;
that it is grounded in our capacity to feel pity, to feel grief.

I know it matters absolutely, and is lovelier than the blue hour
on arbutus and mountain ash.

Radical

It's not that I shy away from the anguish and the hurt, it's that they don't continue to surprise me. His disclosures stunned me. They could not be assimilated in one go. Yet the action of beauty when I was in that place of grief is the revelatory thing. The discovery that, through the qualities of colour and light, through the music and architecture of words, there is a means to express the self at its most fractured and fleeting and a place to exist untrammelled – that was seismic, that was and remains, new.

What Held Me

Tom

My arms are loosely wreathed around you. Leaning back against me, you have a three-year-old's insatiable appetite for play. My two hands pat and catch at yours. Laughing, you swat them away. We are sitting in front of the lobster pots, turquoise and seaweed green, at Brandon Point. Mount Brandon rises above us. The wind washes a salt breeze across the close of a summer day.

Dan

We are in Peggy's house in Killarney. She is trying to determine whom you most resemble from those, much-loved, who came before you. Her mind made up, she hands you back to me. As I take you, my fingertips almost meet one another at the back. I register just how narrow your chest is. Yet, at the same time, I can feel how, within your infant frame, your heart beats, steadily, assuredly.

Like two hands, you held me.

If Ever

If ever they were
        I almost forget now
                they are
                        mine;

the one in Paris
      on Rue Turgot,
           the other, out west,
                  listening to Beach House.

I conjure each voice
        as night falls;
              fold their names
                    into boulevards
                        and sunflowers.

Hope

Look out at dusk to the west of Bcharre,
from the small basilica with its red-tiled tower.
All is hushed around you. Mist on the vineyards.
Smoke rising from a few houses below.
A dog's bark rings out across the gorge
and the great hollows of air, slung across,
catch the rebounding sound. The opening hills
are hands that waft you. There is so much hope
in the view. I would wish to be ushered
by the Qadisha valley which the cedars
of Lebanon call home: though it's the sunset,
the day's end, you gaze at, to all who are
harboured by this sacred landscape
its breath is refuge, its face is dawn.

Maple-serrated

A crimson leaf has fallen from next door's liquidambar,
sugared, star-like, with maple-serrated edges.
A stranger to this muffled world, this dusk of a November.
I place it – red, waxy, vibrant – on a blue enamel plate.

Shape does not have to be seen with an outline around it.
Shapes can be read as mere changes of colour.
Again, the Bonnard words return.
Again, they indicate the way.

Out of the window, the unindividuated world
is beginning to crystallise. Where before
all was blurred, now, things settle into discreteness,
into specific trees and roof tops.

I can see niches and textures; layers and details,
refined like sugar, resolve into distinctness and touch.
It has come back again, the separation which permits
a relationship between the self and the world.

The Dance

Shakespeare's sonnets, their slow movement, their give and take, helped me understand the process. As he came into recovery, I came to understand the dance, the time it needs, its measured grace; how those who have wronged must step forward, express remorse, then you who have been wronged can move forward also. The dance of atonement, of reparation. And so it unfolds, step by step, turn by turn.

And yet sometimes I would snag on those cautious reciprocities. Sometimes I would long for the paradigm shift you find in so many of the sonnets when, after all the courteous toing and froing, the poem reframes itself and makes reference to a higher logic; that moment when, within the poem's charged compass, you feel you touch a truth,

My deepest sense, how hard true sorrow hits

I am thinking again that though I have suffered, he also has suffered; I am thinking again that suffering cannot be weighed or compared, just met with compassion, and acknowledged.

Grey

A few years later he told me that as he struggled to break free of addiction, his belief that my love was still there – I had said when he asked is it over, that I didn't know, 'You didn't say it was over,' he told me after, 'which meant everything' – that possibility that I could still love him was what pulled him through, what delivered him into recovery.

I had said when he asked is it over, that I didn't know...

At the time, that did not feel a position of strength: tentative, contingent, hampered by provisionality. At the time perhaps the easier answer would have been to be more definitive, to say yes, it is over. Yet I see now that had I adopted a more entrenched position, it would have significantly prescribed his response. It would have ruled out what in fact unfolded, a more nuanced kind of growth.

April 1794

Her skirt is a vial of light. The gathered organza swings, it clings to her form, as she crosses the room swiftly, lifting the pearl-grey hemline clear of the ground. She takes the shackled hands, presses them to her lips, sinks to the floor. As she does so, the dress streams out around her. Its metallic threads trap and refract the firelight, stirring a rare notion of comfort in the cold dawn. The year is 1794 and they are man and wife, he Camille Desmoulins, she, Lucile Desmoulins, *née* Laridon-Duplessis. She has come here at his final request to say goodbye, and, despite all that has happened between them, in this, their last hour, they assert their deep, unbreakable bond.

The interlinked chains of his handcuffs. The interlinked threads of her silk gown. The force that links one atom to another in the crystal matrix. Like these, they are bound. And even death, which will come to him first, will not separate them.

The guard is impatient; Camille has followed his wife and is now kneeling. The guard tries to haul him up. The choreography is awkward, uncertain. They are not in synchrony. He rises. She rises. He is ahead of her then behind, she seems to be the first one standing, but no, he is.

The lives of the Desmoulins were tempestuous, their deaths, brutal. Yet, when I imagine this meeting, it's not in their lives and deaths that I find the connection. It's in the way I see their bodies moving in those last moments together. In that stumbling fall and rise, those fumbled attempts to hold hands, in the way that they are out of step yet attuned, motivated by faith not reason is the image of the love that enabled us to come through.

Love

A mild day in spring. White blossom, light rain. A concrete church off the Holloway road. The sun's rays through clear glass soften the sober walls. I'm standing at a lectern skimming the reading for the lunchtime mass. It's quiet, people just beginning to filter in. I'm pregnant with Dan – he's a bump under my duffle coat – and I've arrived late as, in due course, so will he. I don't have time to read over the text properly.

And then the words from Corinthians rise independently and take flight. 'Love' falls like the gentlest of chords, the lightest of showers of spring rain; wherever it alights – on benches of polished wood, on fresh sprigs of hawthorn and forsythia – every growing thing, every made thing, is rendered new. The clear, ancient words express truths which, as they occur, are felt to be both infinitely old and preternaturally new: that love is not resentful, that love takes no pleasure in other peoples' sins but delights in the truth, that love is always ready to trust and to hope, that love does not come to an end.

It's as though a universe comes into being made of the stuff of love, made of atoms and molecules of love; as if, in every sound – a child's cry, the susurration of the leaves, fountains' laughter – love speaks. In the immense night, distant scintillations are other, love, moons, other, love, stars. Love drowns in colour the chalk brushstroke of the Milky Way because, for all its otherness, love cannot be expressed in terms other than its own.

And even now, when I am a long way away from my encounter with those words in St Gabriel's church and when a number of my childhood beliefs have vanished, I still feel love's power, how it is infinitely capacious. Its terms continue to expand.

December 1574

I think of them, Teresa of Avila and John of the Cross
their fingernails rimmed in dirt
trudging through the broken roads of a northern landscape
under a night sky freighted with diamonds.

Pulling their cloaks of coarse wool tight
they are bracing themselves against the sleet and ice
of a Spanish winter.
They are the odd couple, she 52, he just 25 when they meet.

Both of Jewish extraction, they share a stubborn charisma,
a reforming zeal.
They are driven to expunge the corruption
in the Carmelite order.

Each will go on to be loved and admired
but also outcast, ridiculed, hounded,
incarcerated, whipped.
They will live one step ahead of the Inquisition.

She had a vision of a crystal castle
a radiant sanctuary
the soul's dwelling place
deep within each of us.

She wrote *The Interior Castle* in 1577 in Toledo.
Inside the crystal castle are seven chambers.
Each marks a different stage in spiritual development.
The outermost rooms contain evil spirits

vying to beat the traveller back.
But a voice of infinite tenderness
calls out to the pilgrim soul
and persuades them to journey on.

Further within, a keener apprehension;
bright fragrances,
the sweetness of meadow-grass,
the complex perfume of old roses.

Actuality of a different order.
The journey ends at the innermost room
made entirely of crystal.
Here, the pilgrim is reunited with their God.

Life for the Spanish mystics
is fundamentally the journey of the soul.
Is it this conviction that creates in them
so mesmeric a language of longing?

The important thing is not to think much but to love much, St Teresa of Avila.

Minerals Gallery, Natural History Museum, London

As a child I would come to this dark, vaulted space to escape the heat of the city. I'd rest my forehead on the display case's cool, brass frame and peer through the glass at the shimmering prisms. It wasn't just the rarity of the names that captivated me – peridot, beryl, carnelian – nor where those names came from – opal, Sanskrit for precious stone; zircon, Farsi for golden – which swept me away to distant times and places; it wasn't even for the intensity of the colours – though, was there ever a blue like azurite, and what is colour anyway but spheres of silica splitting the light?

It wasn't just to marvel at the nineteenth-century collectors who showed me the wealth under my own soil – gold nuggets from Wicklow, crystals, leaf-green, from Cornwall, grey from the Mendip Hills, deep yellow from Derbyshire; it wasn't even for the thrill of the different expressions of the crystalline forms – one of my favourites – a spray of ice-white splinters, like needles of glass. No; it was something to do with looking into the heart of earth and deep into time, at a mystery that held within it the promise of a pattern. And it was for that one special crystal, a milky quartz, and within that, a purple lustre, what is known as the ghost amethyst.

I look at it now, again, and it is for me a pledge; it urges me to wait, like the crystal that lies in darkness waits until the earth's crust cracks and the sun spills into its blind underworld releasing a torrent of brilliance and colour. It is the conviction that something as yet opaque, unformed, such as, perhaps, this experience, can contain within itself a kind of beauty, and that beauty like love is transformative.

ACKNOWLEDGEMENTS

To my family, who unstintingly supported this publication, my deepest thanks and love.

My gratitude also to Peter Straus and Neil Astley for your belief. Thank you to my earliest mentors, Don Paterson and Bernard O'Donoghue. And to Pam Lehrer, Nick Hornby, Pete Stevenson, Amanda Posey, Joanna Secker Walker and Charlotte Kelly, heartfelt thanks for your wisdom, stellar support and advice.

Acknowledgements are due to the editors of *Wild Court* and *Dressing for Vesuvius* (Templar Press) where versions of some poems first appeared, and to the following academic journals and websites: *Journal of the Academy of Social Sciences*; *American Society of Addiction Medicine*; *Journal of Drug and Alcohol Dependence*; *The Cambridge Handbook of Substance and Behavioral Addiction*; U.S National Institutes of Health; Hazelden Betty Ford Foundation; Psychiatry and Behavioural Health Learning Network; Dr David Sack, Dr Gabor Maté, Sharon Martin, LCSW; psychiatryinstitute.com; scientificamerican.com.

I am indebted to the poets J.H. Prynne (*Poems*, Bloodaxe Books, 2015) and Avi Sharon, translator of C.P. Cavafy's *Selected Poems* (Penguin Classics, 2008) for the enduring inspiration of their work.